Uncommon
Sense

from the Writings of
Howard Zinn

Uncommon
Sense

from the Writings of
Howard Zinn

Selected and Introduced by
Dean Birkenkamp and Wanda Rhudy

Paradigm Publishers
Boulder • London

Published in the Critical Narrative Series, edited by Donaldo Macedo.

View other titles in this series at www.paradigmpublishers.com

Published in the United States by Paradigm Publishers, 3360 Mitchell Lane Suite E, Boulder, CO 80301 USA.

Paradigm Publishers is the trade name of Birkenkamp & Company, LLC, Dean Birkenkamp, President and Publisher.

Library of Congress Cataloging-in-Publication Data

Zinn, Howard, 1922–
  Uncommon sense from the writings of Howard Zinn / selected and introduced by Dean Birkenkamp and Wanda Rhudy.
     p. cm. — (Critical narrative series)
  Includes bibliographical references.
  ISBN 978-1-59451-713-6 (jacketed hardcover : alk. paper)
  1. Zinn, Howard, 1922—Political and social views. I. Birkenkamp, Dean. II. Rhudy, Wanda. III. Title.
  E175.5.Z56Z56 2009
  973'.07202—dc22

                                                                2008050025

Printed and bound in the United States of America on acid-free paper that meets the standards of the American National Standard for Permanence of Paper for Printed Library Materials.

Designed and Typeset by Straight Creek Bookmakers.

13 12 11 10 09   1 2 3 4 5

Contents

Preface

This book has its inspiration in a remark made by a college student, about twenty years old. She was among the hundreds milling in the hallways, hoping to enter the overfilled, 1,500-seat Glen Miller Ballroom at the University of Colorado on a December night in 2006. Like her, we were among the unlucky many stranded outside the ballroom, blocked from entry to Howard Zinn's speech by a line of police (not his favorite mode of "crowd control"). Several hundred of us stayed in the halls, hoping against the unlikely possibility that some of the more fortunate in the ballroom eventually would vacate their seats.

Nearly an hour after the speech commenced, some of us still lingered in the hallways and just talked—about Bush and his war, about the sixties, about Howard Zinn and our disappointment at not hearing him speak.

The young woman (we'll never know her name) said brightly, "He just has a way of saying things that is so memorable, he writes like nobody else."

We were thinking of her words later when we were able to get into an audio-only room set up with large speakers. There we savored the wisdom in Professor Zinn's words, impromptu now in the customary Q & A aftermath of the speech.

Later that evening we spent two hours with Professor Zinn over a late-night snack at his hotel. Joining us was David Barsamian, the Alternative Radio impresario who has interviewed and broadcast Zinn more than any other journalist. We learned from Howard, still youthful at eighty-four years old, that Boulder was his last stop on his last speaking tour—"if I keep my promise to my family," he said with his usual wry humor. For this reason, and many others—his inspiring words, the energy and persistence of the youthful crowds—it seemed a momentous night.

In case Howard keeps his promise, we thought it prudent to assemble this book. The book's quotations are selected from scores of writings over a span of six decades. All are drawn from detailed narratives written about specific events, places, people, or topics. Readers acquainted with Zinn's writings will notice some familiar phrases. They will also appreciate many more that are new to them. Even readers broadly knowledgeable of his corpus will find that the reading of these statements of principle, isolated from specific narratives, and juxtaposed—we hope—in some sensible order, brings new and added meaning to his words.

Howard Zinn has been famous as a historian, speaker, playwright, progressive, debunker, humorist, teacher, and activist. Perhaps this book shows that he should be equally known as a philosopher. As we selected these quotations, we marveled at the wisdom and power of his writings and his consistency of vision—ever probing and expanding—throughout sixty years of writing. Like the best philosophers, he possesses an instinct for human decency and human nature that forms the essence of his critiques of all the powerful institutional forces of government, justice, war, democracy, and more.

Thus the collection could be seen as Professor Zinn's statement of political and moral philosophy. Unlike the books of many philosophers, this is not a long, ponderous treatise for the reader to endure. Instead it is a work of vivid history and living thought, reflecting the life of this man of deep convictions and risk-taking activism. It is a small book handy at the bed stand late at night, when the mind seeks depth, assurance, and optimism. We hope readers will savor and appreciate his quotations as much as we did while assembling them. We hope, too, that the book will serve as an inspiration for personal direction and action.

—Dean Birkenkamp and Wanda Rhudy
Boulder and Montrose, Colorado

History

*H*istory is not inevitably useful. It can bind us or free us.

The Politics of History

⌇

When we compel the past to speak, we want neither the gibberish of total recall nor the nostalgia of fond memories; we would like the past to speak wisely to our present needs.

New Deal Thought

⌇

Recalling the rhetoric of the past, and measuring it against the actual past, may enable us to see through our current bamboozlement, where the reality is still unfolding, and the discrepancies still not apparent.

The Politics of History

⌇

If you can decide what's in people's history and what's left out, you can order their thinking. You can order their values. You can in effect organize their brains by controlling their knowledge.

Failure to Quit

History can help our struggles, if not conclusively, then at least suggestively. History can disabuse us of the idea that the government's interests and the people's interests are the same.

A Power Governments Cannot Suppress

There is an underside to every age about which history does not often speak, because history is written from records left by the privileged. We learn about politics from the political leaders, about economics from the entrepreneurs, about slavery from the plantation owners, about the thinking of an age from its intellectual elite.

It is the victors who give names to the wars, and the satisfied who give labels to the ages.

LaGuardia in Congress

Knowledge has a social origin and social use. It comes out of a divided, embattled world, and is poured into such a world. It is not neutral either in origin or effect.

Secrecy, Archives, and the Public Interest & *The Zinn Reader*

Education becomes most rich and alive when it confronts the reality of moral conflict in the world.

You Can't Be Neutral on a Moving Train

When I taught American history, I ignored the canon of the traditional textbook, in which the heroic figures were mostly presidents, generals, and industrialists. In those texts, wars were treated as problems in military strategy and not in morality; Christopher Columbus, Andrew Jackson, and Theodore Roosevelt were treated as heroes in the march of democracy, with not a word from the objects of their violence. I suggested that we approach Columbus and Jackson from the perspective of their victims, that we look at the magnificent feat of the transcontinental railroad from the viewpoint of the Irish and Chinese laborers who, in building it, died by the thousands.

How Free Is Higher Education? & The Zinn Reader

It was easy to detect the control of the German scholars or the Russian scholars, but much harder to recognize that the high school texts of our own country have fostered jingoism, war heroes, the Sambo approach to the black man, the vision of the Indian as savage, and the notion that white Western Civilization is the cultural, humanistic summit of man's time on earth.

Secrecy, Archives, and the Public Interest & The Zinn Reader

A veil is drawn over the lives of many Americans ... the sounds of prosperity drown out all else, and the voices of the well-off dominate history.

The Politics of History

It was a Harvard professor, Henry Kissinger, who was a strategist of the secret bombing of peasant villages in Cambodia.

Going back a bit in history, it was our most educated president, Woodrow Wilson, a historian himself, a Ph.D. and former president of Princeton, who bombarded the Mexican coast, killing more than one hundred innocent people, because the Mexican government refused to salute the American flag. It was Harvard-educated John Kennedy, author of two books on history, who presided over the American invasion of Cuba and the lies that accompanied it.

What did Kennedy or Wilson learn from all that history they absorbed in the best universities in America? What did the American people learn, in their high school history texts, to put up with these leaders?

Objections to Objectivity

America's future is linked to how we understand our past. For this reason, writing about history, for me, is never a neutral act.

A Power Governments Cannot Suppress

Anyone reading history should understand from the start that there is no such thing as impartial history. All written history is partial in two senses. It is partial in that it is only a tiny *part* of what really happened. That is a limitation that can never be overcome. And it is partial in that it inevitably takes sides, by what it includes or omits, what it emphasizes or deemphasizes. It may do this openly or deceptively, consciously or subconsciously.

The chief problem in historical honesty is not outright lying. It is omission or de-emphasis of important data. The definition of *important*, of course, depends on one's values.

Declarations of Independence

Consider how much attention is given in historical writing to military affairs—to wars and battles—and how many of our heroes are military heroes. And consider also how little attention is given to antiwar movements and to those who struggled against the idiocy of war.

Declarations of Independence

How shall we read the story of the Ludlow Massacre? As another "interesting" event of the past? Or as supporting evidence for an analysis of that long *present* which spans 1914 and 1970. If it is read narrowly, as an incident in the history of the trade union movement and the coal industry, then it is an angry splotch in the past, fading rapidly amidst new events. If it is read as a commentary on a larger question—the relationship of government to corporate power and of both to movements of social protest—then we are dealing with the present. Then we see a set of characteristics which have persisted, not only in American history, but in the history of all nations.

The Politics of History

All historians, by their writing, have some effect on the present social situation, whether they choose to be presentists or not. Therefore the real choice is not between shaping the world or not, but between doing it deliberately or unconsciously.

History as a Private Enterprise

If a historian lies, someone will soon find him out. If he is irrelevant, this is harder to deal with. We have accepted truth as criterion, and we will rush to invoke it, but we have not yet accepted relevance.

History as a Private Enterprise

By writing history, we are engaging in an act which (through the reader) has consequences, large or small, on behalf of humane values or in opposition to them.

The Politics of History

I never wanted to be the kind of historian who goes into the archives and you never hear from him again.

Artists in Times of War

If you do not know some important things about history, then it's as if you were born yesterday.

Howard Zinn on Democratic Education

Everyone does need to learn history, the kind that does not put its main emphasis on knowing presidents and statutes and Supreme Court decisions, but inspires a new generation to resist the madness of governments trying to carve the world and our minds into their spheres of influence.

Objections to Objectivity

As a result of omitting, or downplaying, the importance of social movements of the people in our history—the actions of abolitionists, labor leaders, radicals, feminists, and pacifists—a fundamental principle of democracy is undermined: the principle that it is the citizenry, rather than the government, that is the ultimate source of power and the locomotive that pulls the train of government in the direction of equality and justice. Such histories create a passive and subordinate citizenry.

Declarations of Independence

I have two proposals for archivists: One, that they engage in a campaign to open all government documents to the public. If there are rare exceptions, let the burden of proof be on those who claim them, not as now on the citizen who wants information. And two, that they take the trouble to compile a whole new world of documentary material, about the lives, desires, needs of ordinary people. Both of these proposals are in keeping with the spirit of democracy, which demands that the population know what the government is doing, and that the condition, the grievances, the will of the underclasses become a force in the nation.

Secrecy, Archives, and the Public Interest & *The Zinn Reader*

We all know individuals—most of them unsung, unrecognized—who have, often in the most modest ways, spoken out or acted on their beliefs for a more egalitarian, more just, peace-loving society.

To ward off alienation and gloom, it is only necessary to remember the unremembered heroes of the past and to look around us for the unnoticed heroes of the present.

Unsung Heroes

When our government, our media, and our institutions of higher learning select certain events for remembering and ignore others, we have the responsibility to supply the missing information. Just telling untold truths has a powerful effect, for people with ordinary common sense may then begin asking themselves and others: "What shall we do?"

The Massacres of History

History cannot provide confirmation that something better is inevitable; but it can uncover evidence that it is conceivable.

The Politics of History

The historian too often moves back a hundred years into a moral framework barbarian by modern standards and thinks inside it, while the radical shakes the rafters of this framework at the risk of his life.

Abolitionists and Freedom Riders & *The Zinn Reader*

To refuse to be instruments of social control in an essentially undemocratic society, to begin to play some small part in the creation of a real democracy: these are worthy jobs for historians, for archivists, for us all.

Secrecy, Archives, and the Public Interest & *The Zinn Reader*

It is paradoxical that historians, presumably blessed with perspective, should judge the radical from within the narrow moral base of the radical's own period, while the radical assesses his immediate society from the vantage point of a future, better era.

Abolitionists and Freedom Riders & *The Zinn Reader*

Surely history does not start anew with each decade. The roots of one era branch and flower in subsequent eras. Human beings, writings, invisible transmitters of all kinds, carry messages across the generations. I try to be pessimistic, to keep up with some of my friends. But I think back over the decades, and look around. And then, it seems to me that the future is not certain, but it is possible.

Failure to Quit

In rethinking our history, we are not just looking at the past but at the present, and we are trying to look at it from the point of view of those who have been left out of the benefits of so-called civilizations. It is a simple but profoundly important thing we are trying to accomplish, to look at the world from other points of view. We need to do that as we come into the twenty-first century, if we want this new century to be different, if we want it to be not an American century, or a Western century, or a white century, or a male century, or any nation's or any group's century but a century for the human race.

Howard Zinn on Democratic Education

Government

The obligation that people feel to one another goes back to the very beginning of human history, as a natural, spontaneous act in human relations. Obligation to government, however, is not natural. It must be taught to every generation.

Declarations of Independence

The more widespread education is in a society, the more mystification is required to conceal what is wrong; church, school, and the written word work together for that concealment. This is not the work of a conspiracy; the privileged of society are as much victims of the going mythology as the teachers, priests, and journalists who spread it. All simply do what comes naturally, and what comes naturally is to say what has always been said, to believe what has always been believed.

The Politics of History

We can reasonably conclude that how we *think* is not just mildly interesting, not just a subject for intellectual debate, but a matter of life and death.

If those in charge of our society—politicians, corporate executives, and owners of press and television—can dominate our ideas, they will be secure in their power. They will not need soldiers patrolling the streets. We will control ourselves.

Declarations of Independence

Adoration of law is an essential part of the education and training of citizens in the modern state, and it is common both to the totalitarian states of this century and to those that consider themselves "liberal" and "democratic," including the United States. "Law and order" is the guiding principle for all powerful nation-states.

Postwar America

To give people a choice between two different parties and allow them, in a period of rebellion, to choose the slightly more democratic one was an ingenious mode of control.

A People's History of the United States

In our election-obsessed culture, everything else going on in the world—war, hunger, official brutality, sickness, the violence of everyday life for huge numbers of people—is swept out of the way while the media covers every volley of the candidates. Thus, the superficial crowds out the meaningful, and this is very useful for those who do not want citizens to look beyond the surface of the system. Hidden by the contest of the candidates are real issues of race, class, war, and peace, which the public is not supposed to think about.

Tennis on the Titanic

Totalitarian states love voting. You get people to the polls and they register their approval.

The Problem Is Civil Obedience

Ambiguity has always been useful to those who run societies. It joins a working set of rules and beliefs necessary to keep the system going with a set of ideals that promise something better in the future and soften the harshness of the present.

Postwar America

The government may try to deceive the people, and the newspapers and television may do the same, but the truth has a way of coming out. The truth has a power greater than a hundred lies.

Against Discouragement & *The Zinn Reader*
(2005 Spelman College Commencement Address)

When the citizens begin to suspect they have been deceived and withdraw their support, government loses its legitimacy and its power.

A Power Governments Cannot Suppress

It is a common occurrence in American politics that critics of a certain policy, while fervently declaring their allegiance to moral principle, nevertheless say they can "understand" the reluctance of the President to act on such principle because of the "realities" of politics, that he cannot "afford" (a word I always associated with dire poverty and not with the occupant of the White House) to go against "public opinion." This is almost always a feeble rationalization for a deep lack of principle.

The Zinn Reader

In the never-ending contest between authority and liberty that goes on in every society, the agencies of government, at their best, are still on the side of authority.

Disobedience and Democracy

The decision apparatus on the dropping of the atomic bomb was a perfect example of that dispersed responsibility so characteristic of modern bureaucracy, where an infinite chain of policy-makers, committees, advisers, and administrators make it impossible to determine who is accountable. By comparison, the sly double action of the

Inquisition—the church holding the trial, the state carrying out the execution—was primitive.

Postwar America

"Big government" in itself is hardly the issue. That is here to stay. The only question is: whom will it serve?

Big Government for Whom?

The Constitution ... illustrates the complexity of the American system: that it serves the interest of a wealthy elite, but also does enough for small property owners, for middle-income mechanics and farmers, to build a broad base of support. The slightly prosperous people who make up this base of support are buffers against the blacks, the Indians, the very poor whites. They enable the elite to keep control with a minimum of coercion, a maximum of law— all made palatable by the fanfare of patriotism and unity.

A People's History of the United States

Ironically (in view of the customary assumption that the legal system guards us against anarchy), it is the laws, either by what they provide as they are passed or by what they permit when they are not passed, which contribute to the anarchy of the economic order. They either permit or subsidize the unfettered spoliation of natural resources; they permit, indeed pay for, the production of dangerous things—poisons, guns, bombs. The allocation of the nation's colossal wealth to the production of either weapons or junk takes place not contrary to law but through a vast network of contractual arrangements.

The Conspiracy of Law & The Zinn Reader

We clearly cannot expect the Bill of Rights to be defended by government officials. So it will have to be defended by the people.

Failure to Quit

We subsidize everything in the military—the buildings, the weapons, the transport systems, and the personnel—and pay for it with public funds. We plan for what is needed and it all comes out of the national budget, paid for by taxes. We have a kind of socialism for military needs and capitalism for civilian needs.

Declarations of Independence

The modern liberal capitalist state, by its essential economic and political characteristics, tends to intensify and expand aggressive warfare. It justifies its actions with its own appealing rhetoric, finding successive, specific epithets for "the enemy," and decorating its objectives with talk of liberty, democracy, and, above all, peace.

Postwar America

Are not nations, operating in this tumultuous world, comparable to gangs inside the nation—seeking to enforce law and order in their own limited sphere, without considering law and order in their relations with others? When nations ignore international agreements at will, are they not contributing to gang warfare in the world?

Disobedience and Democracy

When we ... define terrorism as the killing of innocent people for some presumed political purpose, then you find that all sorts of nations, as well as individuals and groups, have engaged in terrorism.

Artists in Times of War

We judge ourselves by our ideals; others by their actions. It is a great convenience.

Vietnam: Setting the Moral Equation

If people and nations can only react on the basis of the most cynical interpretations of the others' conduct, the world doesn't have a chance.

The Prisoners: A Bit of Contemporary History

The romantic aura surrounding sociopolitical theories—the enthusiasm for "socialism," "fascism," "democracy," "liberalism"—has obscured the fact that all ideologies in modern times have been morally limited by national boundaries. This has enabled political leaders to pass off external conflicts over *national* power as conflicts between ideologies, that is, between good and evil.

Postwar America

It does not take too much study of modern history to conclude that nations as a lot tend to be vicious.

My work in American history led to another idea: that there is no necessary relationship between liberalism in domestic policy and humaneness in foreign policy. Some of our most grotesquely immoral deeds have been committed by "liberals." Take Andrew Jackson's murderous attitude toward the Indians in the bloody Trail of Tears, or Progressive Theodore Roosevelt's bullying activities in the Caribbean. Take Woodrow Wilson's behavior towards Haiti and Mexico and his carrying the nation, for reasons still inexplicable, into the pointless savagery of the First World War.

Vietnam: The Logic of Withdrawal

Foreign policy is conducted regardless of popular vote, in the presence of a sheep-like Congress. The voter is as helpless in foreign policy as someone watching with binoculars from a mountaintop while a murder is being committed on another mountaintop.

Disobedience and Democracy

People who are being bombed around the world, or people who are dying as the result of preventable illness, do not vote in American elections. If our political system is not sensitive to human suffering in this country where there are not votes to be counted—the homeless, the imprisoned, the very poor—how can we expect it to care a whit about people a thousand miles from our voting booths, however miserable their situation?

Delusion 2000: How the Candidates View the World

Does morality stop at the water's edge? Is it not precisely one of the requirements of our century that we begin applying in the world those moral precepts we insist on at home?

Disobedience and Democracy

To believe in democracy was to believe in the principles of the Declaration of Independence—that government is an artificial creation, established by the people to defend the equal right of everyone to life, liberty, and the pursuit of happiness. I interpreted "everyone" to include men, women, and children all over the world, who have a right to life not to be taken away by their own government or by ours.

You Can't Be Neutral on a Moving Train

One of the crucial values that the left must embrace is a value of international solidarity and equality across national lines. That's very important, because it changes everything if you begin to understand that the lives of children in other countries are equivalent to the lives of children in our country.

The Future of History

I wake up in the morning, read the newspaper, and feel that we are an occupied country, that some alien group has taken over. I wake up thinking: The U.S. is in the grip of a President surrounded by thugs in suits who care nothing about human life abroad or here, who care nothing about freedom abroad or here, who care nothing about what happens to the earth, the water, or the air, or what kind of world will be inherited by our children and grandchildren.

"Introduction" to *Dear President Bush*

It hasn't been Congress or the president or the Supreme Court who has initiated acts to remedy racial inequality or economic injustice, or to do something about the government going to war. It's always taken the actions of citizens and actions of civil disobedience to bring these issues to national attention and finally force the president, Congress, and the Supreme Court to begin to move.

Howard Zinn on Democratic Education

We need to engage in whatever nonviolent actions appeal to us. There is no act too small, no act too bold. The history of social change is the history of millions of actions, small and large, coming together at critical points to create a power that governments cannot suppress.

An Occupied Country

The Constitution has nothing about the right of people to breathe fresh air or to live in a decent house or to have medical care or to make enough money or to work not too many hours.... Whatever was gained in that way was gained through an enormously rich, complex history of labor struggles in this country.

Second Thoughts on the First Amendment

Let's resist the characteristically American trick of passing off fundamental criticism by pointing to a few reforms.

Secrecy, Archives, and the Public Interest & *The Zinn Reader*

Exactly at that moment when we have begun to suspect that law is congealed injustice, that the existing order hides an everyday violence against body and spirit, that our political structure is fossilized, and that the noise of change—however scary—may be necessary, a cry rises for "law and order." Such a moment becomes a crucial test of whether the society will sink back to a spurious safety or leap forward to its own freshening.

Disobedience and Democracy

Democracy must improve itself constantly or decay.

Disobedience and Democracy

What normally operates day by day is the quiet dominance of certain ideas, the ideas we are expected to hold by our neighbors, our employers, and our political leaders; the ones we quickly learn are the most acceptable. The result is an obedient, acquiescent, passive citizenry—a situation that is deadly to democracy.

If one day we decide to reexamine these beliefs and realize they do not come naturally out of our innermost feelings or spontaneous desires, are not the result of independent thought on our part, and, indeed, do not match the real world as we experience it, then we have come to an important turning point in life. Then we find ourselves examining, and confronting, American ideology.

Declarations of Independence

The citizen's job, I believe, is to declare firmly what he thinks is right.

Vietnam: The Logic of Withdrawal

New definitions of old terms could become a part of the common vocabulary. The old definitions have misled us and caused monstrous harm.

The word *security*, for instance, would take on a new meaning; the health and well-being of people, which is the greatest strength and most lasting security a nation can have....

The word *defense* would mean, not the waging of war and the accumulation of weapons, but the united actions of people against tyranny, using every ingenious device of nonviolent resistance.

Democracy would mean the right of people everywhere to determine for themselves, rather than have political leaders decide for them, how they will defend themselves, how they will make themselves secure, and how they will achieve justice and freedom.

Patriotism would mean not blind obedience to a nation's leaders, but a commitment to help one's neighbors and to help anyone, regardless of race or nationality, achieve a decent life.

Declarations of Independence

War and Peace

*A*t its worst, war has been mass slaughter without even the saving grace of a definable social goal.

The Healthful Use of Power & *The Zinn Reader*

Once an initial judgment has been made that a war is just, there is a tendency to stop thinking, to assume then that everything done on behalf of victory is morally acceptable.... The beneficent nature of a government is assumed to give rightness to the wars it wages.

Declarations of Independence

There's no ideological reason, no territorial reason that can justify the cruelty of war. The means of war have reached the point where they overwhelm any possible decent ends.

The Future of History

It remains to be seen how many people in our time will make that journey from war to nonviolent action against war. It is the great challenge of our time: How to achieve justice, with struggle, but without war.

Declarations of Independence

It is a problem of the corruption of human intelligence, enabling our leaders to create plausible reasons for monstrous acts, to exhort citizens to accept those reasons, and to train soldiers to follow orders. So long as that continues, we will need to refute those reasons and resist those exhortations.

The Bombs of August

Should not the real motivations of governments be scrutinized? They always claim to be fighting for democracy, for liberty, against aggression, to end all wars—but is that not a handy way to mobilize a population to support war, indeed, absolutely necessary because people do not *instinctively* want to fight?

You Can't Be Neutral on a Moving Train

There is endless room for more wars, with an endless supply of reasons ready to justify them.

The Bombs of August

The people who fight the wars are not the people that benefit from the wars.

Artists in Times of War

It is a long story, the betrayal of the very ones sent to kill and die in wars. When soldiers realize this, they rebel. In the Civil War there was deep resentment that the rich could buy their way out of service, and that financiers like J. P. Morgan were profiting as the bodies piled up on the battlefields. The black soldiers who joined the Union army and were decisive in the victory came home to poverty and racism.

Soldiers returning from World War I, many of them crippled and shell-shocked, were hit hard, barely a dozen years after the end of the war, by the Depression. Unemployed, their families hungry, they descended on Washington—20,000 of them, from every part of the country. They set up tents across the Potomac from the Capitol and demanded that Congress pay the bonuses it had promised.

Instead, the army was called out, and the veterans were fired on, tear gassed, and dispersed.

The Ultimate Betrayal

Innocent and well-meaning people—of whom I considered myself one—are capable of the most brutal acts and the most self-righteous excuses, whether they be Germans, Japanese, Russians, or Americans. Later I was trained as a historian and learned that our country is capable of moral absurdities.

Vietnam: The Logic of Withdrawal

"Any means to an end" is a totalitarian philosophy, one that is shared by all nations that make war.

The Bombs of August

It becomes difficult to sustain the claim that a war is just when both sides commit atrocities, unless one wants to argue that their atrocities are worse than ours.

Declarations of Independence

The moral failures of other nations [have] to be seen not in isolation, but against our own failures.

Vietnam: The Logic of Withdrawal

It seems that however moral is the cause that initiates a war (in the minds of the public, in the mouths of the politicians), it is in the nature of war to corrupt that morality until the rule becomes "An eye for an eye, a tooth for a tooth," and soon it is not a matter of equivalence, but indiscriminate revenge.

Declarations of Independence

It is the old human story, the little boy nurtured by his family on the Biblical exhortation Thou Shalt Not Kill, watching his father return, gun still smoking from a mission of murder.

Of Fish and Fishermen & *The Zinn Reader*

American presidents in time of war have pointed to the qualities of the American system as evidence for the justness of the cause. Woodrow Wilson and Franklin Roosevelt were liberals, which gave credence to their words exalting the two world wars, just as the liberalism of Truman made going into Korea more acceptable and the idealism of Kennedy's New Frontier and Johnson's Great Society gave an early glow of righteousness to the war in Vietnam.

Declarations of Independence

War remains the instrument of the state. All that reformers can do is put some moral baggage on its train.

Abolitionists and Freedom Riders & *The Zinn Reader*

If the world is destroyed, it will be a white-collar crime, done in a business-like way, by large numbers of individuals involved in a chain of actions, each one having a touch of innocence.

Dow Shalt Not Kill

More and more in our time, the mass production of massive evil requires an enormously complicated division of labor. No one is positively responsible for the horror that ensues. But everyone is negatively responsible, because anyone can throw a wrench into the machinery. Not quite, of course—because only a few people have wrenches. The rest have only their hands and feet. That is, the power to interfere with the terrible progression is distributed unevenly, and therefore the sacrifice required varies, according to one's means. In that odd perversion of the natural which we call society the greater one's capability for interference, the less urgent is the need to interfere.

It is the immediate victims—or tomorrow's—who have the greatest need, and the fewest wrenches. They must use their bodies (which may explain why rebellion is a rare phenomenon). This may suggest to those of us who have a bit more than our bare hands, and at least a small interest in stopping the machine, that we might play a peculiar role in breaking the social stalemate.

This may require resisting a false crusade—or refusing one or another expedition in a true one. But always, it means refusing to be transfixed by the actions of other people, the truths of other times. It means acting on what we feel and think, here, now, for human flesh and sense, against the abstractions of duty and obedience.

The Politics of History

In the 400 years following the era of Machiavelli and More, making war more humane became the preoccupation of certain liberal "realists." Hugo Grotius, writing a century after More, proposed laws to govern the waging of war (*Concerning the Law of War and Peace*). The beginning of the twentieth century saw international conferences at The Hague in the Netherlands and at Geneva in Switzerland which drew up agreements on how to wage war.

These realistic approaches, however, had little effect on the reality of war. Rather than becoming more controlled, war became more uncontrolled and more deadly, using more horrible means and killing more noncombatants than ever before in the history of mankind.

Declarations of Independence

World War I gave war a bad name. Until World War II came along.

Declarations of Independence

Perhaps the worst consequence of World War II is that it kept alive the idea that war could be just.

Declarations of Independence

Up to the hydrogen bomb, it was still possible to weigh cost and consequence. Now we can throw away the scales, for it should be clear to any rational and humane person that there is no piece of territory (not Berlin or Viet Nam or Hungary), there is no social system yet put into operation anywhere by man (not socialism or capitalism or whatever) which is worth the consequence of atomic war.

The Healthful Use of Power & *The Zinn Reader*

I had no idea what the explosion of the atomic bomb had done to the men, women, and children of Hiroshima. It was abstract and distant, as were the deaths of the people from the bombs I had dropped in Europe from a height of six miles; I was unable to see anything below, there was no visible blood, and there were no audible screams. And I knew nothing of the imminence of a Japanese surrender. It was only later when I read John Hersey's *Hiroshima*, when I read the testimony of Japanese survivors, and when I studied the history of the decision to drop the bomb that I was outraged by what had been done.

Declarations of Independence

Harry Truman lied to us and the world when he said the bomb dropped on Hiroshima was dropped on "a military target."

Howard Zinn on War

In the face of the manifest unpredictability of social phenomena, all of history's excuses for war and preparation for war—self-defense, national security, freedom, justice, stopping aggression—can no longer be accepted. Massive violence, whether in war or internal upheaval, cannot be justified by any end, however noble, *because no outcome is sure.*

Optimistic Uncertainty & The Zinn Reader

Some generals objected, but were overruled by civilians. The technology crowded out moral considerations. Once the planes existed, targets had to be found.

Declarations of Independence

The Vietnam War gave war a bad name.

Declarations of Independence

Early in 1966, a new pacification technique was developed by American soldiers. It involved surrounding a village, killing as many young men as could be found, and then taking away the women and children by helicopter. The Americans called this procedure "Operation County Fair."

Vietnam: The Logic of Withdrawal

By late 1966, the United States was spending for the Vietnam war at an annual rate of twenty billion dollars, enough to give every family in South Vietnam (whose normal annual income is not more than several hundred dollars) about $5,000 for the year. Our monthly expenditure for the war exceeds our annual expenditure for the Great Society's poverty program.

Vietnam: The Logic of Withdrawal

By the 1960s, my old belief in a "just war" was falling apart. I was concluding that while there are certainly vicious enemies of liberty and human rights in the world, war itself is the most vicious of enemies. And that while some societies can rightly claim to be more liberal, more democratic, more humane than others, the difference is not great enough to justify the massive, indiscriminate slaughter of modern warfare.

You Can't Be Neutral on a Moving Train

A Chicago newspaper, asked by a reader if it were true that for every enemy soldier killed in Vietnam the United States was killing six civilians, replied that this was not true; we were killing only four civilians for every soldier.

Vietnam: The Logic of Withdrawal

It is estimated that, in the forty years after 1945, there were 150 wars, with twenty million casualties.

Declarations of Independence

The most powerful nation in the world, producing 60 percent of the world's wealth, using the most advanced weapons known to military science short of atomic bombs, has been unable to defeat an army of peasants, at first armed with homemade and captured weapons, then with modern firearms supplied from outside, but still without an air force, navy, or heavy artillery.

Vietnam: The Logic of Withdrawal

Military power has its limits—limits created by human beings, their sense of justice, and capacity to resist. The United States with 10,000 nuclear weapons could not win in Korea or Vietnam, could not stop a revolution in Cuba or Nicaragua.

A Power Governments Cannot Suppress

They actually gave a Nobel Prize to Henry Kissinger for helping to stop the Vietnam War. Imagine giving one of the architects of the war a prize for helping to stop the war.

Second Thoughts on the First Amendment

I don't want to honor military heroism; that conceals too much death and suffering. I want to honor those who all these years have opposed the horror of war.

Dissent at the War Memorial

My intention is not at all to diminish our compassion for the victims of the terrorism of September 11, but to enlarge that compassion to include the victims of all terrorism, in any place, at any time, whether perpetrated by religious fanatics or American politicians.

A Power Governments Cannot Suppress

We need to realize that the awful scenes of death and suffering we witnessed on 9/11 have been going on in other parts of the world for a long time, and only now can we begin to know what people have gone through, often as a result of our policies. We need to understand how some of those people will go beyond quiet anger to acts of terrorism.

The Old Way of Thinking

We listen with the languor of a people who have never been bombed, who have only been the bombardiers.

Of Fish and Fishermen & *The Zinn Reader*

You can't respond to one terrorist act with war, because then you are engaging in the same kind of actions that terrorists engage in. That thinking goes like this: "Yes, innocent people died, too bad. It was done for an important purpose. It was 'collateral damage.' You must accept 'collateral damage' when you are doing something important." That's how terrorists justify what they do. And that's how nations justify what they do.

Artists in Times of War

I don't want to insist on the distinction between innocent civilians and soldiers who are not innocent. The Iraqi soldiers whom we crushed with bulldozers, toward the end of the First Gulf War in 1991, in what way were they not innocent? The U.S. Army just buried them—buried them—hundreds and hundreds and hundreds of them. What of the Iraqi soldiers the United States mowed down in the so-called Turkey Shoot as they were retreating, already defeated? Who were these soldiers on the other side? They weren't Saddam Hussein. They were just poor young men who had been conscripted.

A Power Governments Cannot Suppress

Getting at the roots of terrorism is complicated. Dropping bombs is simple. It is an old response to what everyone acknowledges is a very new situation. At the core of unspeakable and unjustifiable acts of terrorism are justified grievances felt by millions of people who would not themselves engage in terrorism but from whose ranks violent desperation springs.

A Power Governments Cannot Suppress

The "war on terrorism" is not only a war on innocent people in other countries; it is a war on the people of the U.S.: on our liberties, on our standard of living. The country's wealth is being stolen from the people and handed over to the super-rich. The lives of the young are being stolen.

"Introduction" to *Dear President Bush*

The modest nations of the world don't face the threat of terrorism.

A Power Governments Cannot Suppress

We need to decide against war, no matter what reasons are conjured up by the politicians or the media, because war in our time is always indiscriminate—always a war against innocents, a war against children. War is terrorism, magnified hundreds of times.

The Old Way of Thinking

Today we do not face an expansionist power that demands to be appeased. We ourselves are the expansionist power.

A Power Governments Cannot Suppress

We

Let us be a modest nation; we will then be more secure.

A Power Governments Cannot Suppress

Class

$\mathcal{H}$ow can you have life, liberty, and the pursuit of happiness if you don't have the right to food, housing, and health care?

Artists in Times of War

We very often forget that the Constitution gives political rights but not economic rights. Even those political rights are circumscribed by the nonexistence of economic rights. If you are not wealthy, then your political rights are limited, even though they exist on paper in the Constitution.

Artists in Times of War

How wise Dickens was to make readers feel poverty and cruelty through the fate of children who had not reached the age where the righteous and comfortable classes could accuse them of being responsible for their own misery.

You Can't Be Neutral on a Moving Train

I don't know any film that shows Columbus as what he was, as a man ruled by the capitalist ethic.

Artists in Times of War

If the colonial period of our history constitutes our birth and infancy we were not "born free." We were born amidst slavery, semi-slavery, poverty, land monopoly, class privilege, and class conflict.

The Politics of History

By its domestic and foreign policies, the new American government would maintain the dominant position of the wealthy in society over the next two centuries and beyond. Its legislation would be class legislation, tariffs for the manufacturers, subsidies for the railroads, oil companies, and other giant corporations. Armed force would be used to expel the American Indian tribes from their land, open the West to enterprise, and put down rebellious workers who went out on strike.

A Campaign Without Class

A good society will use incentives—money and time, for example—in all sorts of imaginative ways to bring out the best in people and get the most accomplished for society. But to reward the rich with the incentive of high profits, no matter what work they do or what contribution they make to society, and to punish the poor by withholding the necessities of life (a disincentive, to force them to work) is both unjust and inefficient.

Declarations of Independence

How skillful to tax the middle class to pay for the relief of the poor, building resentment on top of humiliation!

A People's History of the United States

We don't need permission from on high, words approved by the authorities, to tell us that certain truths are self-evident, as the Declaration of Independence put it. That we are all created equal, that we all have rights that cannot be taken from us, the rights to life, liberty, and the pursuit of happiness. And so working people went on strike thousands of times, were beaten and killed on the picket line, until they won an eight-hour day, and a bit of economic security. Women created a national movement that changed the consciousness of millions of people. Gays and lesbians, disabled people, organized, spoke up, declared: we exist, we must be paid attention to. And people began to pay attention.

Failure to Quit

It is possible, reading standard histories, to forget half the population of the country. The explorers were men, the landholders and merchants men, the military figures men. The very invisibility of women, the overlooking of women, is a sign of their submerged status.

A People's History of the United States

Pointing to class divisions in this country has always been dangerous. Thus, when Eugene V. Debs, opposing World War I, told an assembly in Ohio that "the master class has always brought a war, and the subject class has always fought the battle," he was not tolerated. Debs was sentenced to ten years in prison. Oliver Wendell Holmes, in the spirit of patriotic liberalism, affirmed the sentence for a unanimous Supreme Court.

A Campaign Without Class

Amid the smug speeches of the business leaders, and the triumphant clatter of ticker-tape machines, millions of Americans worked all day in mines, factories, and on patches of rented or mortgaged land. In the evening, they read the newspaper or listened to the not-yet-paid-for radio and looked forward to Saturday night, when they might hold their mouths under the national faucet for a few drops of the wild revelry that everyone spoke about. For the fact was that a large section of the American population was living sparely and precariously and, though not jobless and impoverished (as many would be a decade later), were shut out of the high, wild, and prosperous living that marked the upper half of the population.

LaGuardia in Congress

Roosevelt was humane and wise, but he had to react to signs of anger and rebellion in the country. He had seen the Bonus March of veterans to Washington under Hoover.

In his first year, mass strikes—400,000 textile workers out in the south, and New England Longshoremen tied up the whole city of San Francisco. Teamsters took over Minneapolis. The unemployed were organizing, the bootleg miners taking over coalfields, tenants gathering in the cities to stop evictions.

Beyond Voting & *The Zinn Reader*

When the New Deal was over, capitalism remained intact. The rich still controlled the nation's wealth, as well as its laws, courts, police, newspapers, churches, colleges. Enough help had been given to enough people to make Roosevelt a hero to millions, but the same system that had brought depression and crisis—the system of waste, of inequality, of concern for profit over human need—remained.

A People's History of the United States

American capitalism needed international rivalry—and periodic war—to create an artificial community of interest between rich and poor, supplanting the genuine community of interest among the poor that showed itself in sporadic movements.

A People's History of the United States

Our political leaders would prefer us to believe we are one family—me and Exxon, you and Microsoft, the children of the CEOs and the children of the restaurant workers. We must believe our interests are the same. That's why officials speak of going to war "for the national interest," as if it were in *all* our interest.

A Campaign Without Class

In an economy motivated by private corporate profit, the human effects of production are secondary, and social concern is a luxury.

Postwar America

Human happiness seems to depend on the balance of expectations and fulfillment. If there is no possibility of fulfillment, it is socially desirable to reduce expectations.

The Politics of History

Shouldn't it be an elementary rule of civilization that no human being should be deprived of heat or light or cooking fuel because of lack of money? Where does all that gas and electricity come from anyway? From coal, from oil, from the earth, from the stored energy of the sun, shining down for a billion years. Who took it on themselves, in some distant past, to sell the sun to Boston Edison? ... These are life's necessities, like food, air, water. They should not be the private property of corporations, which use them to hold us hostage to the dark, to the cold, until we pay their price.

Who Owns the Sun? & *The Zinn Reader*

To break the hold of corporations over our food, our rent, our work, our lives—to produce things people need, and give everyone useful work to do and distribute the wealth of the country with approximate equality—whether you call it socialism or not, isn't it common sense?

The Secret Word

It's a sad story what's happened to the American labor movement, if you trace it from the IWW especially through the CIO and down to the present day. The labor movement is a victim of the general American culture and the lack of a very strong radical movement in the U.S. It leaves the working people of the U.S. absolutely prone before CBS and NBC and the 6 o'clock news and the glimmers of stuff that gets in newspapers.... When Reagan broke the air controllers' strike, nobody was speaking out against it, nobody was saying to workers all across the country, Don't you recognize? This is your tomorrow.... It's part of the general decline of social consciousness in America.

The Future of History

Control in modern times requires more than force, more than law. It requires that a population dangerously concentrated in cities and factories, whose lives are filled with cause for rebellion, be taught that all is right as it is. And so, the schools, the churches, the popular literature taught that to be rich was a sign of superiority, to be poor a sign of personal failure, and that the only way upward for a poor person was to climb into the ranks of the rich by extraordinary effort and extraordinary luck.

A People's History of the United States

Think of whatever progress has been made in this country for economic justice. Obviously, not enough progress has been made for economic justice, looking around at this country. You have to look around. You have to walk through a whole city. If you walk through half a city you'll be mistaken. You have to walk through a *whole* city and you see the class structure in the United States, the hidden story of American prosperity.

Second Thoughts on the First Amendment

That was my world for the first thirty-three years of my life—the world of unemployment and bad employment, of me and my wife leaving our two- and three-year-olds in the care of others while we went to school or to work. Living most of that time in cramped and unpleasant places, hesitating to call the doctor when the children were sick because we couldn't afford to pay him, finally taking the children to hospital clinics where interns could take care of them. This is the way a large part of the population lives, even in this, the richest country in the world. And when, armed with the proper degrees, I began to move out of that world, becoming a college professor, I never forgot that. I never stopped being class-conscious.

You Can't Be Neutral on a Moving Train

When Chrysler ran out of cash in 1980, the government stepped in to help. (Try that next time you run out of cash.)

Big Government for Whom?

The U.S. political establishment insists that we mustn't talk about class. Only Marxists do that, although thirty years before Marx was born, James Madison, "Father of the Constitution," said that there was an inevitable conflict in society between those who had property and those who did not.

A Campaign Without Class

I note how our political leaders step gingerly around such expressions, how it seems the worst accusation one politician can make about another is that "he appeals to class hostility ... he is setting class against class." Well, class has been set against class in the realities of life for a very long time, and the words will disappear only when the realities of inequity disappear.

You Can't Be Neutral on a Moving Train

The threat of unemployment, always inside the homes of the poor, has spread to white-collar workers, professionals. A college education is no longer a guarantee against joblessness, and a system that cannot offer a future to the young coming out of school is in deep trouble. If it happens only to the children of the poor, the problem is manageable; there are the jails. If it happens to the children of the middle class, things may get out of hand.

A People's History of the United States

Some coming generation perhaps, while paying proper respects to the spirit of the New Deal, may find, as William James put it, "the moral equivalent of war"—in new social goals, new expectations, with imaginative, undoctrinaire experimentation to attain them.

New Deal Thought

If films are made and reach the public, about war, class conflict, and who controls what; and about the history of governmental lies, broken treaties, and official violence; if those stories are told, we might really produce a new generation.

Artists in Times of War

Racism and Resistance

$\mathcal{P}$hysical difference is so gross a stimulus to human beings, cursed as they are by the gift of vision, that once it is latched onto as explanation for difference in personality, intelligence, demeanor, it is terribly difficult to put aside. It becomes an easy substitute for the immensely difficult job of explaining personal and social behavior.

The Southern Mystique

Slavery is over, but its degradation now takes other forms, at the bottom of which is the unspoken belief that the black person is not quite a human being. The recollection of what slavery is like, what slaves are like, helps to attack that belief.

The Politics of History

To be a Negro in the South has, for most Negroes, most of the time, no drastic consequences like beatings or lynchings. But it has, for all Negroes in the South, all of the time, a fundamental hurt which cannot be put into words or statistics. No Negro, even in that minority of wealth and position, can escape the fact that he is a special person, that wherever he goes, whatever he does, he must be conscious of this fact, that his children will bear a special burden on their emotions from the moment they begin to make contact with the outside world.

Abolitionists and Freedom Riders & *The Zinn Reader*

The liberal response to the "race problem" in the United States—that is, to the black uprisings, for black subordination was not a "problem" until blacks went wild in the streets—did not touch the heart of the matter. The heart of the matter was not the lack of laws, or lack of words, or lack of promises. It was insufficient economic resources, the absence of real, direct political power, and surrounding those hard needs—something more subtle and yet enormous—the psychology of racism that inhabited the minds of whites, the acceptance of white superiority so deeply in every aspect of American society that black children might grow up believing it.

Postwar America

It was once thought that slavery had destroyed the black family. And so the black condition was blamed on family frailty, rather than on poverty and prejudice.

A People's History of the United States

The complicity of poor white people in racism ... is a very important issue. It seems to me that complicity can't be understood without showing the intense hardships that poor white people faced in this country, making it easier for them to look for scapegoats for their condition. You have to recognize the problems of white working people in order to understand why they turn racist, because they aren't born racist.

Howard Zinn on Democratic Education

The need for slave control led to an ingenious device, paying poor whites—themselves so troublesome for two hundred years of southern history—to be overseers of black labor and therefore buffers for black hatred.

A People's History of the United States

In the history of labor struggles, you should show how blacks and whites were used against one another, how white workers would go out on strike and then black people, desperate themselves for jobs, would be brought in to replace the white workers, how all-white craft unions excluded black workers, and how all this created murderously intense racial antagonisms.

Howard Zinn on Democratic Education

Hassled whites turn on blacks. Angry blacks retaliate. Will this hostility ever end? Not until black and white people discover together the source of their long feud—an economic system which has deprived them and their children for centuries, to the benefit of, first, the Founding Fathers, and lately, the hundred or so giant corporations that hog the resources of this bountiful country.

When Will the Long Feud End? & *The Zinn Reader*

The relations between whites and blacks in the United States was a microcosm of the relations between Americans and people in other parts of the world.

Howard Zinn on Democratic Education

I think of the poor today, so many of them in the ghettos of the nonwhite, often living a few blocks away from fabulous wealth. I think of the hypocrisy of political leaders, of the control of information through deception, through omission. And of how, all over the world, governments play on national and ethnic hatred.

You Can't Be Neutral on a Moving Train

The dehumanization of the "enemy" has been a necessary accompaniment to wars of conquest. It is easier to explain atrocities if they are committed against infidels or people of an inferior race. Slavery and racial segregation in the United States and European imperialism in Asia and Africa were justified in this way.

Howard Zinn on Democratic Education

The forced passage of millions of black slaves to the New World in the sixteenth, seventeenth, eighteenth and nineteenth centuries was concomitant with the basic features of what we proudly call Western Civilization. Large scale slavery was a product not of the Dark Ages, but of the Renaissance and the Scientific and Commercial Revolutions; it was expanded not by feudal baronies but by the new national states; its most powerful impetus was not manorialism but capitalism; it was justified not by pagan ritual but by Christian doctrine (by the spokesmen for the Protestant Reformation as well as the Church of Rome).

The Politics of History

Slavery ... was ended not because of an upsurge of moral resentment in the North, or an insistence on the principle of freedom by the federal government. It was ended because the political and economic interests of the slaveholders clashed with those of the Northern politicians and business interests to the point of war. Expediency, flavored with morality, brought emancipation, and only after prolonged, unrelenting pressure on Lincoln by Abolitionists.

The Politics of History

This is one of the unchanging aspects of our self-evaluation—that we mention the Negro with proper lamentation, and then put him in brackets while we make our total judgment of American civilization. Both slavery and segregation have always been treated as special phenomena, to be mentioned then forgotten, because they spoil all estimates about democracy, freedom, and equality in this country.

The Politics of History

Given the national government's long and persistent history of neglect in using its powers to protect the black person, that neglect could hardly be regarded as some temporary aberration from the real system, but rather as the system itself, the operating reality of liberal government in contradistinction to its rhetorical claims.

Postwar America

The Supreme Court might make equalitarian rulings, the Congress might pass civil-rights laws, the president might make stirring speeches about the dignity of man, but the black man on the ghetto street or on the country road was still at the mercy of the white man—in uniform or out—and the power of the government was not available to

protect him. The situation that obtained during slavery—
the physical helplessness of the black before the white—was
still being maintained in the post-slavery world.

Postwar America

Racism, ostensibly, was one reason the war was fought—to
wipe out the race doctrines of Hitler. But in the United
States, the idea of white supremacy in the North and South
proved greater than the libertarian enthusiasm generated by
the war. The most striking and bitter irony was that black
soldiers fought in the war in segregated units, in separate
and unequal situations.

Postwar America

My air crew sailed to England on the *Queen Mary*. That
elegant passenger liner had been converted into a troop
ship. There were 16,000 men aboard, and 4,000 of them
were black. The whites had quarters on deck and just below deck. The blacks were housed separately, deep in the
hold of the ship, around the engine room, in the darkest,
dirtiest sections. Meals were taken in four shifts (except
for the officers, who ate in prewar *Queen Mary* style in a
chandeliered ballroom—the war was not being fought to

disturb class privilege), and the blacks had to wait until three shifts of whites had finished eating.

Declarations of Independence

The civil-rights movement illuminated the hypocrisy of the liberal promise. It made overt, and recorded on television for the world to see, an old daily fact of American life: that a black person who protested his condition, or moved one step out of line, would be arrested, or beaten, or inundated with water hoses, or killed, and the national government of the United States—the most powerful government in the world—would not act to save him.

Postwar America

There is a rough analogy between Lincoln's insistence (in that famous letter to Horace Greeley) that he was more concerned with *union* than with slavery, and Kennedy's unspoken but obvious preoccupation with *law and order* above either desegregation or the right of free assembly.

Kennedy: The Reluctant Emancipator & *The Zinn Reader*

Are we not more obligated to achieve justice than to obey the law?

Declarations of Independence

The premise of liberal reform, that "someone," the white reformer, would solve the problems of the black man, was false. Now especially among the young black people, the most essential element of a real democracy had begun to take hold—that an oppressed people can depend on no one but themselves to move that long distance, past all defenses, to genuine dignity.

Postwar America

The sit-ins marked a turning point for the Negro American, subordinate for three hundred years. He was rebelling now, not with the blind, terrible, understandable hatred of the slave revolts, but with skill in organization, sophistication in tactics, and an unassailable moral position. With these went a ferocious refusal to retreat. What had been an orderly, inch-by-inch advance via legal processes now became a revolution in which unarmed regiments marched from one objective to another with bewildering speed.

SNCC: The New Abolitionists

The advent of the Freedom Rides in 1961—busloads of integrated Northerners riding through the most backward areas of the deep South in direct and shocking violation of local law and custom—made the sit-ins seem a rather moderate affair. And the emergence of the militantly anti-white Black Muslims made the integrationist advocates of nonviolence seem even more moderate. "Extremism" is still a relative term.

Abolitionists and Freedom Riders & The Zinn Reader

The summer of 1964 saw a massive effort against racial segregation in Mississippi, when a thousand people from all over the country, mostly white college students, joined local black Mississippians in Freedom Summer. Those weeks were filled with courageous attempts to break down racial barriers in what black people considered the most murderous of states. There were repeated acts of violence against the civil rights workers, culminating in the murder of one black and two white civil rights workers.... Throughout, the federal government played its usual role of observing, but not acting, in effect abnegating its responsibility to enforce constitutional rights everywhere in the nation.

The South Revisited

The continued physical helplessness of the black in the face of either official brutality in violating the Constitution or official laxity in enforcing it was only the most obvious fact about a larger truth. That truth was the general failure of the whole liberal parade of court decisions, laws, and presidential declarations in affecting the basic subordinate position of the black in the United States. It was this failure that perhaps best explains the burst of black militancy after 1965.

Postwar America

Black and white have always been morally intertwined in American history, even when physically separated, even when playing out the roles of subordinate and superior. The new black consciousness of the sixties, the activism, the militancy, the radicalism, could not leave untouched the sensibilities of whites, many of whom were moved, some easily, some through great inner turbulence, to rethink their attitudes and their behavior. Conflict shakes up old ways, it hastens reorientations, and the race conflicts of this postwar period were intense.

Postwar America

In the area of racial equality, from Lincoln to Kennedy, the man at the pinnacle of national political power has chosen to play the cautious game of responding, inch by inch, to the powerful push of "extremists," "trouble-makers," and "radicals." For Lincoln it was the abolitionists; for Kennedy the sit-inners and Freedom Riders.

Abolitionists and Freedom Riders & *The Zinn Reader*

Progress toward racial equality in the United States is certain, but this is because agitators, radicals and "extremists"—black and white together—are giving the United States its only living reminder that it was once a revolutionary nation.

Abolitionists and Freedom Riders & *The Zinn Reader*

Race consciousness is hollow, its formidable-looking exterior is membrane-thin and is worn away by simple acts of touch, the touching of human beings in contact that is massive, equal and prolonged. The brightness of the physical difference impression is relative; it stands out in that darkness created by segregated living, and is quickly lost in the galaxy of sense impressions that come from being with a person day-in, day-out.

The Southern Mystique

Law and Justice

$\mathcal{T}$he test of justification for an act is not its legality but its morality.

Declarations of Independence

It wasn't "we the people" who established the Constitution: it was fifty-five white, prosperous men who established the Constitution. There were people left out of it, people ignored by it, and the Constitution was not set up in order to benefit all of the people as one classless group but to benefit the upper classes of that time, to benefit the bondholders and the slaveholders and the land speculators and the manufacturers.

Howard Zinn on Democratic Education

The rule of law does not do away with the unequal distribution of wealth and power, but reinforces that inequality with the authority of law. It allocates wealth and poverty (through taxes and appropriations) but in such complicated and indirect ways as to leave the victim bewildered.

Declarations of Independence

Early in the rule of the new government of the United States, Congress passed and President John Adams signed the Sedition Act, which made it a crime to say anything "false, scandalous, or malicious" against the government, Congress, or the president, with intent to "bring them into disrepute." Ironically, it came seven years after the First Amendment was added to the Constitution, as if to state the lesson early on: In the real world, constitutional promises are one thing and political realities are another.

Artists in Times of War

We should know by now that we cannot count on the courts, the Congress, or the presidency, to assure us the freedom to speak, to write, to assemble, and to petition.

Declarations of Independence

Freedom of expression does not depend on the First Amendment.

Second Thoughts on the First Amendment

Our right to free expression is not determined by the words of the Constitution or the decisions of the Supreme Court, but by who has the *power* in the immediate situation where we want to exercise our rights.

Declarations of Independence

On the eve of war, in 1940, Congress passed, and Roosevelt signed, the Alien Registration Act, known as the Smith Act, which made it a crime to advocate the overthrow of the government by force and violence in speech or writing, or to "affiliate" with organizations urging such action. It was therefore made a crime to advocate what Thomas Jefferson and the Founding Fathers had advocated in the Declaration of Independence.

Postwar America

We in America are so far removed from our own revolutionary tradition, and the abolitionist tradition, and also from the reality of suffering among other people, that we consider as unpardonable transgressions of law and order what are really mild acts, measured against the existing evils.

Disobedience and Democracy

It is a deception of the citizenry to claim that the "rule of law" has replaced the "rule of men." It is still men (women are mostly kept out of the process) who enact the laws, who sit on the bench and interpret them, who occupy the White House or the Governor's mansion, and have the job of enforcing them.

Declarations of Independence

What was done before—exploiting the poor, sending the young to war, and putting troublesome people in dungeons—is still done, except that this no longer seems to be the arbitrary action of the feudal lord or the king; it now has the authority of neutral, impersonal law.

Declarations of Independence

More justifiable laws (for free speech, against rape or murder) stand in the front ranks as a noble façade concealing a huge body of law which maintains the present property and power arrangements of the society. Buried in the mass is a much smaller body of law which stands guard against those who would rebel in an organized way against these arrangements.

The Conspiracy of Law & *The Zinn Reader*

Uncertainty about which actions will be protected by the courts and which will not is itself intimidating, in the same way that a helpless prisoner, subjected to alternating acts of cruelty and kindness, is terrorized more effectively than a person who knows what he faces.

Postwar America

Equal Justice Under Law is the slogan one sees on the marble pillars of the courthouse. And there is nothing in the words of the Constitution or the laws to indicate that anyone gets special treatment. They look as if they apply to everyone. But in the actual administration of the laws are rich and poor treated equally? Blacks and whites? Foreign born and natives? Conservatives and radicals? Private citizens and government officials?

Declarations of Independence

Selective enforcement of the law is not a departure from law. It is *legal*.

The Conspiracy of Law & *The Zinn Reader*

The critical deprivations of liberty never get to the courts. They are settled "out of court" in the way that most such settlements are determined—by who is bigger and richer and can afford to wait.

Failure to Quit

Many defendants who insist on their innocence are induced to plead guilty simply because they are told that if they plead not guilty and are convicted by a jury their sentence will be much heavier. The persuasive argument used here is that defendants run the risk of additional punishment for insisting on too much due process of law when the courts and lawyers are already very busy.

Postwar America

Legal training is a wonderful thing; it enables you to explain the unexplainable, defend the indefensible, and rationalize the irrational.

Failure to Quit

A jury "of one's peers" is one of the myths of the legal system. A jury is always a more orthodox body than any defendant brought before it; for blacks it is usually a whiter group, for poor people, a more prosperous group.

You Can't Be Neutral on a Moving Train

The courtroom, one of the supposed bastions of democracy, is essentially a tyranny. The judge is monarch. He is in control of the evidence, the witnesses, the questions, and the interpretation of law.

Declarations of Independence

Definition of what is moral coincides almost exactly with what is constitutional, and what is constitutional is what the Supreme Court decides. Thus is morality reduced to law, and law to the current opinions of the Court.

Disobedience and Democracy

The record of the Supreme Court in our history hardly supplies evidence that it is free of nationalist bias, or that it is willing to subject the United States itself to the same scrutiny for lawbreaking that the individual citizen must face.

Disobedience and Democracy

The courts should stand for the law sometimes, for justice always.

Disobedience and Democracy

Even if the Court should become a staunch supporter of free speech in the streets, how much meaning would its endorsement have so long as the police have the physical power to arrest anyone whose speech disturbs them? The arrested person might eventually get a reversal by the courts—if he is willing to spend some time in jail, tens of thousands of dollars in legal fees, and several years waiting for his case to come before the Supreme Court. In other words, the protection of the Constitution is a distant one; the immediate power over free speech is with those who possess club and gun on the spot where exercise of the freedom is being sought.

Postwar America

The existence of a law, or a constitutional provision, on the books tells us little about its effect.

The Conspiracy of Law & The Zinn Reader

In a world where justice is maldistributed, historically and now, there is no such thing as a "neutral" or "representative" recapitulation of the facts, any more than one is dealing "equally" with a starving beggar and a millionaire by giving each a piece of bread. The condition of the recipient is crucial in determining whether the distribution is just.

History as a Private Enterprise

The poor are the ones who inhabit the jails. Is it because they commit the most crimes? They are the ones who most often *get caught* committing crimes, because they have the least resources for getting away with their crimes, for covering up their deeds, the least resources for paying fines, arranging bail, hiring first-class counsel, making the right contacts.

Justice in Everyday Life

The huge proportion of poor people in jail for crimes against property suggests that prisons are inevitable counterparts of banks.... So long as we have a system that breeds fierce and unequal competition for scarce resources (although it is not the only system that requires imprisonment), some steel bars will be needed to protect money, and others to confine human beings.

They Were Expendable

To decide if a practice is torture, shall we ask the torturers or shall we ask the tortured? Are not certain conditions, by their nature, definable only by the people who suffer them?

Justice in Everyday Life

Is not the death penalty a kind of terror waged by the state, one death at a time, an attempt to instill fear and obedience in the population? That is the perverted sense of morality which now rules and will go on ruling, until Americans decide that it will no longer be tolerated.

A Power Governments Cannot Suppress

There are societies that do not pretend to be "civilized"— military dictatorships and totalitarian states—and execute their victims without ceremony. Then there are nations like the United States, whose claim to be civilized rests on the fact that its punishments are legitimized by a complex set of judicial procedures. This is called "due process," despite the fact that each step in this process is tainted by racial prejudice, class bias, or political discrimination.

A Power Governments Cannot Suppress

Obviously race has played a critical factor in who gets executed in this country. Therefore we can't allow capital punishment, because it violates the equal protection of the law, the Fourteenth Amendment.

The Future of History

To define an evil in terms of a specific group, where such an evil is not inherent in the group but capable of springing up anywhere, is to remove responsibility from ourselves. It is what we have always done in criminal law, which is based on revenge for past acts, rather than a desire to make constructive social changes.

The Politics of History

Prisons cannot be reformed, any more than slavery can be reformed. They have to be abolished.

Justice in Everyday Life

The responsibility for what we see around us belongs to the legal system itself, not to the deviations from it.

The Conspiracy of Law & *The Zinn Reader*

Neutrality is a fiction in an unneutral world. There are victims, there are executioners, and there are bystanders.

The Politics of History

We should insist on the principle that all victims are created equal.

Disobedience and Democracy

The Constitution, it seems, cannot protect us from the greatest threat of all: being considered less than a person in our daily lives.

Justice in Everyday Life

When it is the *normal* functioning of society which produces poverty, racism, imperial conquest, injustice, oligarchy—and when this society functions normally through an elaborate framework of law—this suggests that what is wrong is not aberrational, not a departure from law and convention, but is rather bound up with that system of law, indeed, operates through it.

The Conspiracy of Law & The Zinn Reader

What would seem to be an inherent ethic of stability turns out to be quite undependable, as we find the rule of law in practice creating certain kinds of stability at the expense of other kinds: national at the expense of international, civil at the expense of personal; or as we find that a "peace"

enforced by the rule of law is purchased at the price of future disorder.

The Conspiracy of Law & *The Zinn Reader*

The same modern civilization which has given us unjust laws has given us great ideals. We need to learn how to violate these laws in such a way as to realize those ideals.

Each of us, depending on where we are in the social structure, must draw his own existential conclusion on what to do.

The Conspiracy of Law & *The Zinn Reader*

Marxism and Anarchism

$\mathcal{T}$he value of human welfare comes second to "the foundation of law and order," which is another way of saying that the perpetuation of the status quo, with only the mildest of disturbance and the slimmest of reforms, is the supreme value.

Disobedience and Democracy

There is, on the part of many people, just a general reluctance to weaken the spirit of obedience to law, a fear that "it will lead to anarchy," or to a "break down of law and order." ... That is the same basically conservative impulse which once saw minimum wage laws as leading to socialism, or bus desegregation leading to intermarriage, or Communism in Vietnam leading to world Communism.

Disobedience and Democracy

Patriotism does not mean support for your government. It means, as Mark Twain said, support for your country.

The feminist anarchist Emma Goldman said, at roughly the same time as Twain, that she loved the country but not the government.

Artists in Times of War

"Life would be chaos." If we allow disobedience to law we will have anarchy. That idea is inculcated in the population of every country. The accepted phrase is "law and order." ... It is a phrase that has appeal for most citizens, who, unless they themselves have a powerful grievance against authority, are afraid of disorder.

Declarations of Independence

When people idolize the "rule of law" it is usually because they not only minimize the existing grievances, but magnify the scariness of the act of civil disobedience.

Disobedience and Democracy

When people idolize the "rule of law" it is usually because they not only minimize the existing grievances, but magnify the scariness of the act of civil disobedience.

To do so would be to "take the law into your own hands." That is exactly what civil disobedience is: the temporary taking of the law into one's own hands, in order to declare what the law *should* be. It is a declaration that there is an incongruence between the law and human values, and that sometimes this can only be publicized by breaking the law.

Dow Shalt Not Kill & *The Zinn Reader*

We are asked, "What if everyone disobeyed the law?" But a better question is, "What if everyone obeyed the law?" And the answer to that question is much easier to come by, because we have a lot of empirical evidence about what happens if everyone obeys the law, or if even most people obey the law.

The Problem Is Civil Obedience

Protest beyond the law is not a departure from democracy; it is absolutely essential to it. It is a corrective to the sluggishness of "the proper channels," a way of breaking through passages blocked by tradition and prejudice. It is disruptive and troublesome, but it is a necessary disruption, a healthy troublesomeness.

Declarations of Independence

Civil disobedience can be accomplished by two forms: violating a law which is obnoxious; or symbolically enacting a law which is urgently needed. When Negroes sat-in at lunch counters, they were engaging in both forms: they violated state laws on segregation and trespassing; they were also symbolically enacting a public accommodations law even before it was written into the Civil Rights Act of 1964.

Dow Shalt Not Kill

Surely, peace, stability and order are desirable. Chaos and violence are not. But stability and order are not the only desirable conditions of social life. There is also *justice,* meaning the fair treatment of all human beings, the equal right of all people to freedom and prosperity. Absolute obedience to law may bring order temporarily, but it may not bring justice.

Declarations of Independence

How real is the social peace which harbors drug addiction, alcoholism, mental illness, crimes of violence, and all those thousands of instances of despair which will never be entered in the hospital records or the police blotter because they have been safely contained by society's instruments of control? The nation remains unperturbed by the disorder within each individual, and is quite pleased, so long as that does not break out and reveal itself by a "disturbance of the peace."

Disobedience and Democracy

It's a strange thing, we think that the law brings order. Law doesn't. How do we know that law does not bring order? Look around us. We live under the rule of law. Notice how much order we have? People say we have to worry about civil disobedience because it will lead to anarchy. Take a look at the present world in which the rule of law obtains. This is the closest to what is called anarchy in the popular mind—confusion, chaos, international banditry.

The Problem Is Civil Obedience

There is a tendency to think that what we see in the present moment we will continue to see. We forget how often in this century we have been astonished by the sudden crumbling of institutions, by extraordinary changes in people's thoughts, by unexpected eruptions of rebellion against tyrannies, by the quick collapse of systems of power that seemed invincible.

You Can't Be Neutral on a Moving Train

To me the idea of civil disobedience is to really enhance democracy, to give people out of power a weapon with which to batter against the pillars of the society.

Howard Zinn on Democratic Education

As soon as you say the topic is civil disobedience, you are saying our *problem* is civil disobedience. That is *not* our problem. Our problem is civil *obedience*. Our problem is the numbers of people all over the world who have obeyed the dictates of the leaders of their government and have gone to war, and millions have been killed because of this obedience. Our problem is that people are obedient all over the world, in the face of poverty and starvation and stupidity, and war, and cruelty.

The Problem Is Civil Obedience

Coming to the faculty of Boston University in the fall of 1964, I was introduced to another new faculty member whose field was philosophy. Learning that I was joining the political science department, he asked: And what is your political philosophy?" I replied, half seriously, "Anarchism." He looked at me sharply and said: "Impossible."

Emma: A Play in Two Acts

Not long ago, someone referred to me publicly as a "Marxist professor." I felt a bit honored. A "Marxist" means a tough guy, a person of formidable politics, someone not to be trifled with, someone who knows the difference between absolute and relative surplus value, and what is commodity fetishism, and refuses to buy it.

Nothing Human Is Alien to Me

The Communist Manifesto had a profound effect on me, because everything I saw in my own life, the life of my parents, and the conditions in the United States in 1939 seemed to be explained, put into a historical context, and placed under a powerful analytical light.

"Foreword" to *Marx in Soho*

When Marx talked about what a socialist society would look like, he certainly did not expect that a socialist society would set up gulags, would imprison dissidents and shoot not just capitalists, but fellow revolutionaries, as was done in both the Soviet Union and China. So the police state and the totalitarian nature of the Soviet Union were very foreign to Marx and Engels. They saw the dictatorship of the proletariat as a temporary phenomenon during which the socialist character of society would become more and more communal, more and more democratic, and that the state, as they said, would become less and less necessary. Marx and Engels talked in *The Communist Manifesto* about their aim being the free development of the individual.

The Future of History

Disillusionment with the Soviet Union did not diminish my belief in socialism, any more than disillusionment with the United States government lessened my belief in democracy.

You Can't Be Neutral on a Moving Train

To me it is interesting that socialism in this country was at its most influential before a Soviet Union existed. Because then the people could, without the imposition of some foreign, distorted example, take a look at the ideas of socialism. It made a lot of sense to them. They could see Eugene Debs and Mother Jones and Emma Goldman and Jack London and Lincoln Steffens and see obviously admirable people in the U.S. who had turned to socialism because they saw what capitalism was doing to people. Socialism at that time represented a simple common-sense idea, that you take the wealth of the country and try to use it in a rational and humane way.

The Future of History

I became interested in anarchism for several reasons. One was the growing evidence of the horrors of Stalinism in the Soviet Union, which suggested that the classical Marxian concept of "the dictatorship of the proletariat" needed to be reconsidered. Another was my own experience in the South in the struggle against racial segregation spearheaded by the Student Nonviolent Coordinating Committee. SNCC, without any self-conscious theorizing, acted in accord with anarchist principles: no central authority, grassroots democratic decisionmaking. In the New Left of the 1960s, this was called "participatory democracy."

"Foreword" to *Marx in Soho*

If you look at the laws passed in the United States from the very beginning of the American republic down to the present day, you'll find that most of the legislation passed is class legislation that favors the elite, that favors the rich. You'll find huge subsidies to corporations all through American history. You'll find legislation passed to benefit the railroads, the oil companies, and the merchant marine and very little legislation passed to benefit the poor and the people who desperately need help. So the Law should not be given the holy deference that we are all taught to give it when we grow up and go to school, and it's a profoundly undemocratic idea to say that you should judge what you do according to what the Law says—undemocratic because it divests you as an individual of the right to make a decision yourself about what is right or wrong and it gives all of that power to that small band of legislators who have decided for themselves what is right and what is wrong.

Howard Zinn on Democratic Education

Marxism is not a fixed body of dogma, to be put into big black books or little red books, and memorized, but a set of specific propositions about the modern world which are both tough and tentative, plus a certain vague and yet exhilarating vision of the future, and, more fundamentally, an approach to life, to people, to ourselves, a certain way of thinking about thinking as well as about being. Most of all it is a way of thinking which is intended to promote action.

Marxism and the New Left

In 1893, a terrible year of economic crisis, when children in the cities were dying of hunger and sickness, Emma Goldman addressed a huge demonstration in Union Square, and urged her listeners to invade the food stores and take what they needed for their families—rather than waiting for legislation or petitioning the authorities. This was a vivid illustration of the anarchist principle of "direct action."

Emma: A Play in Two Acts

I think that the history of the United States indicates that the redressing of serious grievances has not been done by the three branches of government that are always paraded before junior high school students and high school students as the essence of democracy.

Howard Zinn on Democratic Education

It is up to the citizenry, those outside of power, to engage in permanent combat with the state, short of violent, escalatory revolution, but beyond the gentility of the ballot-box, to ensure justice, freedom and well being, all those values which virtually the entire world has come to believe in.

The Healthful Use of Power & *The Zinn Reader*

"There is a possibility of choice. Only a possibility, I grant. Nothing is certain. That is now clear. I was too damned certain. Now I know—anything can happen. But people must get off their asses.

Does that sound too radical for you? Remember, to be radical is simply to grasp the root of a problem. And the root is *us.*"

Karl Marx in *Marx in Soho*

Lacking traditional forms of power and wealth, we can only create a force out of what we do have: our assembled selves, our ability to withhold our labor, to withdraw our compliance. Defying authority, we can organize to take hold of what is at hand and rightfully belongs to us— our workplaces, our schools, our communities. And in the midst of struggle—for that is what it will take—we can start right now to construct and endlessly reconstruct human relationships, institutional arrangements, ways of thinking. That, done close to home, inside the small circles of our daily life, might be the beginnings of justice.

Justice in Everyday Life

That is exactly the point of civil disobedience, of a politics of protest—that it is an attempt to bring about revolution- ary social changes without the enormous human toll of suicidal violence or total war, which often fall on a society unwilling to go outside accustomed channels.

Disobedience and Democracy

What we are trying to do, I assume, is really to get back to the principles and aims and spirit of the Declaration of Independence. This spirit is resistance to illegitimate authority and to forces that deprive people of their life and liberty and right to pursue happiness, and therefore under these conditions it urges the right to alter or abolish their current form of government—and the stress has been on abolish. But to establish the principles of the Declaration of Independence we are going to need to go outside the law, to stop obeying the laws that demand killing or that allocate wealth the way it has been done or that put people in jail for petty technical offenses and keep other people out of jail for enormous crimes. My hope is that this kind of spirit will take place not just in this country but in other countries because they all need it. People in all countries need the spirit of disobedience to the state.

The Problem Is Civil Obedience

I do not think civil disobedience is enough; it is a way of protest, but in itself it does not construct a new society. There are many other things that citizens should do to begin to build a new way of life in the midst of the old, to live the way human beings should live—enjoying the fruits of the earth, the warmth of nature and of one another— without hostility, without the artificial separation of religion, or race, or nationalism.

Disobedience and Democracy

Taking Action

$\mathcal{I}$ have come to believe that our lives can be turned in a different direction, our minds adopt a different way of thinking, because of some significant though small event. That belief can be frightening or exhilarating, depending on whether you just contemplate the event or *do* something with it.

You Can't Be Neutral on a Moving Train

As dogma disintegrates, hope appears. Because it seems that human beings, whatever their backgrounds, are more open than we think, that their behavior cannot be confidently predicted from their past, that we are all creatures vulnerable to new thoughts, new attitudes.

And while such vulnerability creates all sorts of possibilities, both good and bad, its very existence is exciting. It means that no human being should be written off, no change in thinking deemed impossible.

You Can't Be Neutral on a Moving Train

It can be important in circumstances where the advantages are so evenly balanced that even the feather-weight of social conviction may tip the decision-making scales.

A Quiet Case of Social Change & *The Zinn Reader*

History is full of instances of successful resistance (although we are not informed very much about this) without violence and against tyranny, by people using strikes, boycotts, propaganda, and a dozen different ingenious forms of struggle.

Declarations of Independence

There is a fable written by German playwright Bertolt Brecht that goes roughly like this: A man living alone answers a knock at the door. When he opens it, he sees in the doorway the powerful body, the cruel face, of The Tyrant. The Tyrant asks, "Will you submit?" The man does not reply. He steps aside. The Tyrant enters and establishes himself in the man's house. The man serves him for years. Then The Tyrant becomes sick from food poisoning. He dies. The man wraps the body, opens the door, gets rid of the body, comes back to his house, closes the door behind him, and says, firmly, "No."

Declarations of Independence

The idea of saviors has been built into the entire culture, beyond politics. We have learned to look to stars, leaders, experts in every field, thus surrendering our own strength, demeaning our own ability, obliterating our own selves.

A People's History of the United States

It is one thing to experiment to discover the best means of achieving a certain objective; it is quite another thing to fail to recognize that objective.

New Deal Thought

Rationality is limited by time, space, and status, which intervene between the individual and the truth. Emotion can liberate it.

Abolitionists and Freedom Riders & *The Zinn Reader*

There is no necessary connection between emotionalism and irrationality. A lie may be calmly uttered, and a truth may be charged with emotion. Emotion can be used to make more rational decisions, if by that we mean decisions based on greater knowledge, for greater knowledge involves not only extension but intensity.

Abolitionists and Freedom Riders & *The Zinn Reader*

The power of a bold idea uttered publicly in defiance of dominant opinion cannot be easily measured. Those special people who speak out in such a way as to shake up not only the self-assurance of their enemies, but the complacency of their friends, are precious catalysts for change.

You Can't Be Neutral on a Moving Train

The observer who is critical of the radical may be subconsciously conjuring the picture of a world peopled only with radicals, a world of incessant shouting, lamenting, and denunciation. But it would be good for him to also imagine a world without any radicals—a placid, static, and evil-ridden world with victims of injustice left to their own devices, a world with the downtrodden friendless. In all ages, it has been first the radical, and only later the moderate, who has held out a hand to men knocked to the ground by the social order.

Abolitionists and Freedom Riders & *The Zinn Reader*

We're living at a time when it becomes even more important to dissent from the establishment and the president, when everybody's crying, "We must unite behind the president." It's exactly at such a time when we need dissenting voices. The irony is that it's exactly in times of war—when you're dealing with life-and–death matters—that you're not supposed to speak. So you have freedom of speech for trivial matters, but not for life-and-death matters. That's a nice working definition of democracy, isn't it?

Artists in Times of War

It seems that women have best been able to make their first escape from the prison of wifeliness, motherhood, femininity, housework, beautification, isolation, when their services have been desperately needed—whether in industry, or in war, or in social movements. Each time practicality pulled the woman out of her prison—in a kind of work-parole program—the attempt was made to push her back once the need was over, and this led to women's struggle for change.

A People's History of the United States

"Extremist" carries a psychological burden when attached to political movements, which it does not bear in other situations. A woman who is extremely beautiful, a man who is extremely kind, a mechanic who is extremely skillful, a child who is extremely healthy—these represent laudable ideals. In politics, however, the label "extremist" carries unfavorable implications.

Abolitionists and Freedom Riders & *The Zinn Reader*

To me one of the cardinal principles in any moral code is the reduction and elimination of violence. The burden of proof in any argument about social tactics should rest on that person who wants to stray from nonviolence.

Disobedience and Democracy

Compromise was not disdained by the abolitionists; they were fully conscious of the fact that the outcome of any social struggle is almost always some form of compromise. But they were also aware of that which every intelligent radical knows: that to compromise in advance is to vitiate at the outset that power for progress which only the radical propels into the debate.

Abolitionists and Freedom Riders & *The Zinn Reader*

I can understand pessimism, but I don't believe in it. It's not simply a matter of faith, but of historical evidence. Not overwhelming evidence, just enough to give hope, because for hope we don't need certainty, only possibility.

Failure to Quit

The bad things that happen are repetitions of bad things that have always happened—war, racism, maltreatment of women, religious and nationalist fanaticism, starvation. The good things that happen are unexpected.

You Can't Be Neutral on a Moving Train

The word "optimism" ... makes me a little uneasy, because it suggests a blithe, slightly sappy whistler in the dark of our time. But I use it anyway, not because I am totally confident that the world will get better, but because I am certain that *only* such confidence can prevent people from giving up the game before all the cards have been played.... To play, to *act*, is to create at least a possibility of changing the world.

Failure to Quit

The struggle for justice should never be abandoned because of the apparent overwhelming power of those who have the guns and the money and who seem invincible in their determination to hold on to it. That apparent power has, again and again, proved vulnerable to human qualities less measurable than bombs and dollars: moral fervor, determination, unity, organization, sacrifice, wit, ingenuity, courage, patience—whether by blacks in Alabama and South Africa, peasants in El Salvador, Nicaragua, and Vietnam, or workers and intellectuals in Poland, Hungary, and the Soviet Union itself. No cold calculation of the balance of power need deter people who are persuaded that their cause is just.

Abolitionists and Freedom Riders & *The Zinn Reader*

I don't mind getting arrested when I have company—and the official charge against us used the language of the old trespass law: "failure to quit the premises." On the letter I got dropping the case (because there were too many of us to deal with) they shortened that charge to "failure to quit."

I think that sums up what it is that has kept the Bill of Rights alive. Not the President or Congress, or the Supreme Court, or the wealthy media. But all those people who have refused to quit, who have insisted on their rights and the rights of others, the rights of all human beings everywhere.

Failure to Quit

Say what you want. What resources do you have to speak out? How many people can you reach? You can get up on a soapbox and no one arrests you, and you reach 200

people. Procter and Gamble, which made the soapbox, has the money to go on the air and reach five million people. Freedom of speech is not just a quality. It's a quantity.

Second Thoughts on the First Amendment

Change in public consciousness starts with low-level discontent, at first vague, with no connection being made between the discontent and the policies of the government. And then the dots begin to connect, indignation increases, and people begin to speak out, organize, and act.

A Power Governments Cannot Suppress

I have never used the word "pacifist" to describe myself, because it suggests something absolute, and I am suspicious of absolutes. I want to leave openings for unpredictable possibilities. There might be situations—and even such strong pacifists as Gandhi and Martin Luther King believed this—when a small, focused act of violence against a monstrous, immediate evil would be justified.

A Power Governments Cannot Suppress

Marx really said this to someone who annoyed him: "I'm not a Marxist!"

Words of Encouragement

From 1964 to 1972, the wealthiest and most powerful nation in the history of the world made a maximum military effort, with everything short of atomic bombs, to defeat a nationalist revolutionary movement in a tiny, peasant country—and failed. When the United States fought in Vietnam, it was organized modern technology versus organized human beings, and the human beings won.

A People's History of the United States

A box cutter can bring down a tower. A poem can build up a movement. A pamphlet can spark a revolution.

"Introduction" to *Dear President Bush*

We hear many glib dismissals of today's college students as being totally preoccupied with money and self. In fact, there is much concern among students with their economic futures—evidence of the failure of the economic system to provide for the young, more than a sign of their indifference to social injustice.

Failure to Quit

When one voice speaks out against the conventional wisdom and is recognized as speaking truth, people are drawn out of their previous silence.

Dissent at the War Memorial

With the sun shining beautifully overhead, the marchers sang, "Free*dom*! Free*dom*! Freedom's coming and it won't be long." Of course it would be long, but did that matter if people were on the move, knowing they were shortening the distance however long it was?

You Can't Be Neutral on a Moving Train

There's a lot of work to be done in speaking up. We need to create that excitement about the issues of the time, excitement about the war, excitement about the misallocation, the waste of the country's wealth on the military. We need information. People have to know things. People have to spread the information. That is a job that all of us have to be engaged in day by day. That's the job of democracy.

Second Thoughts on the First Amendment

A Note
on Sources

We drew from and cited the earliest source we could find for each quote. Under each quote we cite only the main titles of the work in which the quotation originally appeared. Full sources, including subtitles, and additional citations to current reprint editions of some books can be found in the bibliography. Sometimes we use shortened main titles. For example, *Emma: A Play in Two Acts* is listed in the text. In the bibliography the play's entire citation is listed: *Emma: A Play in Two Acts About Emma Goldman, American Anarchist.*

Some Zinn fans may be disappointed if one or more of their favorite quotes do not appear in this collection. Nor is every Zinn article or book represented in these pages. We regret any disappointments and share the feelings. A wealth of quotes remain, untapped, in our notes. We favored thematic chapters of reasonable length so that the reader might savor those offered. And selectivity was necessary as we sought to organize each chapter around some rough logic of unfolding ideas and subthemes.

In a few cases (without changing any of Howard Zinn's words) small liberties were taken so as to tidy the quotation's form. For example, each quote begins with a capitalized letter, even when occasionally we excerpted only the latter part of a sentence.

Bibliography

Books by Howard Zinn

Artists in Times of War and Other Essays. New York: Seven Stories Press, 2003.

Declarations of Independence: Cross-Examining American Ideology, 1st edition. New York: HarperCollins, 1990.

Disobedience and Democracy: Nine Fallacies on Law and Order. New York: Random House, 1968. Reprint edition, Cambridge, MA: South End Press, 2002.

Emma: A Play in Two Acts About Emma Goldman, American Anarchist. Cambridge, MA: South End Press, 1986, 2002.

Failure to Quit: Reflections of an Optimistic Historian. Monroe, ME: Common Courage Press, 1993. Reprint edition, Cambridge, MA: South End Press, 2002.

Howard Zinn on War. New York: Seven Stories Press, 2001.

Justice in Everyday Life: The Way It Really Works (ed.). New York: William Morrow and Company, 1974.

LaGuardia in Congress. Ithaca: Cornell University Press, 1959.

Marx in Soho: A Play on History, 1st edition. Cambridge, MA: South End Press, 1999.

New Deal Thought. Indianapolis: Bobbs-Merrill, 1966.

A People's History of the United States, 1st edition. New York: Harper and Row, 1980.

The Politics of History: With a New Introduction, 2nd edition. Urbana: University of Illinois Press, 1990.

Postwar America: 1945–1971. Indianapolis: Bobbs-Merrill, 1973. Reprint edition, Cambridge, MA: South End Press, 2002.

A Power Governments Cannot Suppress. San Francisco: City Lights, 2007.

SNCC: The New Abolitionists. Boston: Beacon Press, 1964. Reprint edition, Cambridge, MA: South End Press, 2002.

The Southern Mystique, 1st edition. New York: Knopf, 1964. Reprint edition, Cambridge, MA: South End Press, 2002.

Vietnam: The Logic of Withdrawal. Boston: Beacon Press, 1967. Reprint edition, Cambridge, MA: South End Press, 2002.

You Can't Be Neutral on a Moving Train: A Personal History of Our Times. Boston: Beacon Press, 1994.

The Zinn Reader: Writings on Disobedience and Democracy. New York: Seven Stories Press, 1997.

Books Coauthored by Howard Zinn

With David Barsamian. *The Future of History: Interviews with David Barsamian.* Monroe, ME: Common Courage Press, 1999.

With Donaldo Macedo. *Howard Zinn on Democratic Education.* Boulder and London: Paradigm Publishers, 2005.

Articles, Chapters, and Speeches

"Abolitionists and Freedom Riders." *Columbia University Forum.* Summer 1964.*

"Against Discouragement." Spelman College Commencement Address. May 2005.*

"Beyond Voting." *Boston Globe.* 1976.*

"Big Government for Whom?" *The Progressive.* April 1999.

"The Bombs of August." *The Progressive.* 2002.

"A Campaign Without Class." *The Progressive.* 2001.

"The Conspiracy of Law." In *The Rule of Law,* Robert Paul Wolff (ed.). New York: Simon and Schuster, 1971.*

"Delusion 2000: How the Candidates View the World." *The Progressive*. 2002.

"Dissent at the War Memorial." *The Progressive*. 2004.

"Dow Shalt Not Kill." *Jewish Currents*. March 1968.*

"Failure to Quit." *Z Magazine*. June 1988.

"Of Fish and Fishermen." *Ramparts*. 1967.*

"The Healthful Use of Power." *American Journal of Orthopsychiatry*. January 1966.*

"History as a Private Enterprise." In *The Critical Spirit* (the Festschrift for Herbert Marcuse), Kurt H. Wolff and Barrington Moore, Jr. (eds.). Boston: Beacon Press. January 1966.

"How Free Is Higher Education?" *Garnett Center Journal*. New York: Columbia University Press. Summer 1991.*

"Introduction." In Cindy Sheehan's *Dear President Bush*. San Francisco: City Lights, 2006.

"Kennedy: The Reluctant Emancipator." *The Nation*. December 1962.*

"Marxism and the New Left." In *The New Left*, Priscilla Long (ed.). Boston: Porter Sargent, 1969.

"The Massacres of History." *The Progressive*. 1998.

"Nothing Human Is Alien to Me." *Z Magazine*. June 1988.

"Objections to Objectivity." *Z Magazine*. October 1989.

"An Occupied Country." *The Progressive*. October 2003.

"The Old Way of Thinking." *The Progressive*. 2001.

"Optimistic Uncertainty." *Z Magazine*. February 1988.*

"The Prisoners: A Bit of Contemporary History." in *The Politics of History*, 2nd edition. Urbana: University of Illinois Press, 1990.

"The Problem Is Civil Obedience." In *Violence: The Crisis of American Confidence*, Hugh Davis Graham (ed.). Baltimore: Johns Hopkins University Press, 1972.

"A Quiet Case of Social Change." *The Crisis*. October 1959.*

"Second Thoughts on the First Amendment." *The Humanist*. November/December 1991.

"Secrecy, Archives, and the Public Interest." *The Midwestern Archivist*. 1977.*

"The Secret Word." *Boston Globe*. January 24, 1976.

"The South Revisited." *The Nation*. Fall 1965.

"The Southern Mystique." *The American Scholar*. Winter 1963–1964.

"Tennis on the Titanic." ZNet commentary. http://www.zmag.org.
  December 16, 2006.
"They Were Expendable." *Saturday Review.* March 22, 1975.
"The Ultimate Betrayal [Plight of GIs and Veterans]." *The Progres-
  sive.* April 2004.
"Unsung Heroes." *The Progressive.* June 2000.
"Vietnam: The Logic of Withdrawal." *The Nation.* February 1967.
"Vietnam: Setting the Moral Equation. *The Nation.* January 1966.
"When Will the Long Feud End?" *Boston Globe.* September 19,
  1975.*
"Who Owns the Sun?" *Boston Globe.* February 28, 1975.*
"Words of Encouragement." *The Progressive.* September 1999.

*These articles can also be conveniently found in *The Zinn Reader:
Writings on Disobedience and Democracy,* Seven Stories Press, 1997,
sometimes under slightly variant titles.

Acknowledgments

We would like to thank the many publishers who generously agreed to our use of quotations from Howard Zinn's writings.

We also thank Brenda Alderete and Taylor Balthazar for typing hundreds of quotations and helping us organize them for the selection process.

Loving thanks to Susan Jones, Julianna Birkenkamp, and Maya Birkenkamp for accepting the late hours and missed family time; to Chris Carroll for championing. And to Angie Burnham for the magic words.

Special thanks to our editor, Carol Smith, and all of the wonderfully talented staff at Paradigm Publishers.

Foremost, thanks to Howard Zinn for the camaraderie and collaboration.